HOW TO WIN YOUR NCAA TOURNAMENT POOL

ED FENG

TABLE OF CONTENTS

Get your March Madness cheat sheet

As a thank you for purchasing this book, you can get my cheat sheet for filling out your bracket every year.

These results are based on an algorithm I developed while working on my Ph.D. in Chemical Engineering at Stanford University. I discuss this method for rankings teams in the Introduction of this book.

The results in the cheat sheet are optimal for winning a small pool. After reading this book, Chapter 3 in particular, you'll know how to adjust these results for larger pools.

To get your free March Madness cheat sheet, go to thepowerrank.com.

Introduction

You want to win your March Madness pool.

You know the obvious benefits of winning. Money. Ego. Bragging rights for the year.

But perhaps you crave something more, like the thrill of finishing ahead of the office loudmouth, Bob. This lunatic thinks he's skilled at Super Bowl squares even though the numbers get assigned at random (he's won the last two years). You'd like to smack him for his ridiculousness, but office propriety forbids it.

The March Madness pool gives you an opportunity to get back at Bob, but it seems so hard to win. Even the most dedicated fan doesn't have the time to follow the sixty-some teams that make the tourney. This makes it nearly impossible to predict early round upsets.

However, there's a better way to win your March Madness pool than picking upsets at random in the early rounds.

This book offers an analytics and strategy driven approach to winning your March Madness pool. Analytics provides a means to make more accurate predictions than others in your pool. Strategy will let you exploit the biases of others to increase your odds of winning.

The research in this book looks at how this approach has performed over a multitude of past tournaments. This journey reveals the hidden truth behind the optimal way to fill out your bracket.

I first presented this unique approach in 2015. Unsolicited, one of my readers, Ryan Peters, tweeted this before the Final Four: "used your advice for all 3 of my brackets with contrarian champs, duke can win me two different pools. thank you sir." Duke won the tourney, and Ryan didn't hear a peep out of Bob for a month, enjoying the glorious silence.

How to predict tourney games

It's difficult to predict the outcome of tournament games.

First, college basketball gives us a limited number of games each year to evaluate teams. In addition, the differing strength of schedules make this lack of data even worse. For example, Duke plays a much more difficult schedule than Stephen F. Austin.

Second, randomness plays a huge role in the outcome of basketball games. College basketball features the grace and stupidity of hormonal males with an average age around 20. Throw in the randomness of a bouncing basketball, particularly on three point shots, and you get upsets like Mercer over Duke in the Round of 64.

It's not possible to overcome the randomness of college basketball. In fact, it will help us win pools (more on that in the next section). But analytics can help with the lack of data and differing strength of schedule. Let me explain.

In 2008, I was reading a paper on Google's PageRank technology. This algorithm brought order and insight to the complex world of web search. The basic idea was that a website was important if another important website linked to it.

I quickly realized that this applied to sports. Teams are webpages, and games are links between the teams. In sports, teams earn credibility for beating other good teams.

The direct application of PageRank doesn't lead to good tournament predictions. However, I took the core ideas and applied my Ph.D. research at Stanford to develop a new method for ranking teams. These developments allowed me to use margin of victory in games instead of wins and losses as the primary input.

When I first developed this method, I did some NFL predictions and sent an email to some friends. Their encouragement prompted me to look at other sports, including college basketball.

Implementing college basketball was a challenge, as I had to teach my computer how to solve 351 equations simultaneously for 351 variables, one for each team. However, the results were worth it.

Tom Kellogg of Madison, Wisconsin, sent me this email about my tournament predictions: "You'll be glad to know that I have been and continue to be in first place in my family bracket, and yesterday the message board was abuzz with talk of my first 8 picks being perfect. My police officer cousin threatened to subpoena my IP address to make sure I had picked before the games started. I explained my picks and posted a link to The Power Rank website, which prompted my uncle to cry foul about my research methods!"

For the 2002 through 2018 tournaments, I've tested how my pre-tourney predictions fared in over a thousand games. The team favored by my numbers has won 71.2% of games (792-320).

Using analytics for your bracket is much like counting cards in blackjack. In this popular casino game, the odds of winning a hand depend on which cards remain in the deck. By keeping track of dealt cards, people like Jeff Ma, an analytics guru and the inspiration behind the movie *21*, made money off the casinos.

Did Jeff win every hand in blackjack? No. Did he win every time the deck gave him the best chance of winning, like doubling down on 11? No way. However, Jeff won enough that he's no longer welcome to play blackjack in Las Vegas.

In the same way, analytics will not predict every

tournament game. Again, numbers can't overcome the inherent randomness in college basketball. But analytics gives you the best chance to get ahead of the competition.

However, an accurate predictor of games isn't enough to win every pool. You need the right strategy, and here's why.

How to think contrarian

In 2015, Kentucky came roaring into the tournament with an undefeated record.

Coach John Calipari has embraced the one and done era of college basketball in which the best players leave for the NBA after a year. Each season, he deals with a new freshman class of talented but untested players.

However, the 2014-15 season was different for Calipari. Some of his best players from a Final Four team the previous year, like Aaron Harrison and Willie Cauley-Stein, stayed around for another year. Along with this typical stellar recruiting class, Kentucky fielded a deep and experienced team.

Kentucky's dominance and undefeated record inevitably led to a bias among bracket pickers. More people picked Kentucky to win than the numbers merited. And you can exploit this bias to increase your odds of winning your pool.

But first, assume you pick Kentucky as champion in a big pool. My numbers suggested this choice by a wide margin over other teams.

The problem is that many others in your pool also pick Kentucky as champion. If the Wildcats win, you and many others get the 32 points. However, with so many others getting these points, there's a strong chance that one of them gets lucky with low probability upsets in the earlier rounds and beats you.

If the top half of the pool entrants split the pot equally, then Kentucky would be a stellar choice for champion. Your solid picks using analytics in the earlier rounds would almost certainly put you in the money. However, most pools do not work like this. Only the top bracket (or maybe three) win prize money.

To win this type of pool, you need a contrarian strategy. You need to pick a champion with a decent win probability but who is not getting picked as champion in many pools.

It worked for Randy Athay from Lake Havasu City, Arizona, who read the first edition of this book in 2015. "I played 2 contrarians (Arizona & Duke) in a middle size pool. I used your advice in picking the games (rather than waste time looking for sleepers etc.). Going into tonight, I would take 1st with a Duke win or take 3rd with a loss. I was fortunate to win the bigger pot. Much appreciated." Duke won the tourney in 2015.

To understand this contrarian strategy further, consider daily fantasy football. Each week, contestants pick a lineup of players and score points based on statistics like touchdowns and yards gained.

In 50-50 leagues, the top half of participants split the pot equally. In these contests, it makes sense to pick players expected to score a large number of points. For example, you might pick a pre-2015 Peyton Manning as your quarterback. It's similar to picking Kentucky to win the tourney in 2015.

Daily fantasy also offers Guaranteed Prize Pools, contests with thousands of players hoping to win a bigger prize. Only a small fraction of players win money. In these massive contests, a contrarian approach makes sense. In all likelihood, many others in the pool own Peyton Manning. Contrarian thinking implies finding a quarterback that not as many people own but still has a decent chance of scoring a lot of points, like Matt Stafford.

In daily fantasy sports, it's difficult to apply this contrarian strategy. Predicting player performance is hard, and you often have to guess what fraction of pool participants pick a particular player.

Neither of these problems applies to March Madness pools. In the next chapter, I'll show you how analytics can predict tourney win probabilities with reasonable accuracy over a wide range of years. In addition, ESPN publishes data on how many people pick a particular team to win a game. With millions of pool participants, it gives us good statistics on public behavior.

This book uses this analytics and public data to provide reliable estimates of how contrarian strategies perform.

Is this book for you?

In all honesty, this book might not be for you.

You'll be asked to bend your mind and believe ideas that aren't intuitively obvious, like picking a champion in your pool that doesn't have the best chance of winning the tourney.

I'll support these claims with research based on cold, hard data. However, believing in these results also requires a nimbleness of thought.

I'm asking you to believe that if the 2015 tournament happened again, Kentucky would win (even though they didn't win the actual tourney). In fact, they would win more of these simulated tourneys than any other team.

It's not easy for someone new to sports analytics to believe the research in this book. It's much easier to think you know who's going to win the tourney, then search the internet for which 12 seeds to pick in the first round (the latter is a huge waste of time).

But it helps if you've read books like *Moneyball* and *Freakonomics* and buy the idea that data can reveal hidden truths. This book will reveal these truths about winning your NCAA tournament pool. It's a reference book for the smart bracket picker, something to grab every year for a refresher.

You won't win your pool every year. But if you apply the ideas in picking your bracket every year, you'll end up way ahead of loudmouth Bob, king of Super Bowl squares.

1. How to predict the NCAA tournament

In 2012, Amy Nelson of *SB Nation* got interested in my tourney analytics and how they could help her win her pool. She flew out to San Francisco to make a documentary on my research. We met at a sports bar there, in a city on the forefront of technology and innovation.

While I was helping Amy fill out her bracket, her crew interviewed some bar patrons. Four of these clips made the beginning of the documentary. Here's what they said.

There's no way you can predict sports based on mathematics. There's always going to be an upset. There's always going to be a surprise. There always is every year.

You can't quantify which of these guys is going to get nervous and which ones are not.

It's March Madness. You can never predict what's going to happen. That's why it's the madness.

Running numbers on March Madness takes the heart out of it.

Yes, these quotes came from the same city in which many of Google's and Facebook's engineers live.

If you focus on a narrow range of games, they have a point. In 2014, Connecticut entered the tourney as a 7 seed and long shot to win the tourney. The Huskies needed overtime to beat St. Joseph's in the round of 64. Then, out of nowhere, Connecticut won the next five games to win the tournament, an event that no computer or sensible human would have predicted.

In addition, the tournament always features those thrilling upsets the first weekend. In 2013, 15 seed Florida Gulf Coast looked like the Harlem Globetrotters as they won two games and earned a berth in the Sweet 16. Each year, a team seeded 10th or higher makes the second weekend of the tournament.

However, randomness looks different over a longer time horizon.

How often does the higher seeded team win?

From 2002 through 2018, the NCAA tournament has featured 1,112 games. In 1,057 of those games, the opponents had different seeds. (In recent years, the tourney has featured a First Four, a set of four games that feature teams with the same seed. Also, teams with the same seed could potentially meet in the Final Four.) The higher seeded team has won 71.7% of those tournament games (758-299).

Let's stop to appreciate the accuracy of such a simple predictor. Each year, a selection committee, which consists of athletic directors and conference commissioners, assigns a seed to the 60-plus teams that make the tourney. Inclusion on this committee requires no coaching experience or any background in numbers and analytics. Yet over a huge sample of games, the higher seed wins more than two of every three games.

There are always lower seeded teams that defy these odds, and we all love these upsets. In the 2014 tournament, 15 seed Mercer upset 2 seed Duke, and sports bars across the nation exploded in delight as if it started raining $100 bills. It didn't matter that most picked Duke in their pool.

Even better, Kansas entered the 2010 tourney as the clear favorite, as 41.8% of brackets on ESPN picked the Jayhawks to win it all. However, Kansas lost to Northern Iowa in the Round of 32, as Ali Farokhmanesh hit a late three point shot to seal the victory.

You always remember the thrilling upsets, those games in which randomness takes over and slays the big favorite. However, these games are the exception. In the big picture, the favorite usually wins, which makes it worth trying to predict the outcome of the tourney.

These numbers also show the problem with the typical bracket filling advice. Let's see if you've heard this before: The 12 seed has beaten the 5 seed in past tournaments, so look for an upset pick in these games. This advice is flawed for many reasons.

First, the 5 seed has won 67.9% of games over the 12 seed (data from mcubed.net for the 1980 through 2018 tournaments). Remember, the favorite usually wins.

Second, these early round games don't matter much in your pool. Most pools use a scoring system that awards one point for a correct pick in the Round of 64, two points for the Round of 32, and doubling values for each subsequent round. Early round games are inconsequential compared with the championship game that's worth 32 points.

The most important choice in your bracket is the champion. The seeds assigned to teams will not help you with this decision, since four teams get a 1 seed. However, analytics can shed light on this decision through win probability calculations.

How often can analytics predict the tourney winner?

With the growth of sports analytics, many gurus calculate the win probability for each team in the tourney. You might have seen the projections of Nate Silver at FiveThirtyEight or Ken Pomeroy on his college basketball analytics site, kenpom.com.

Here, we'll use my own calculations at The Power Rank since we can look at how these numbers perform over a range of years. Each year, you can find these numbers on an interactive visual on my site, thepowerrank.com.

Calculating tourney win probabilities starts with my college basketball team rankings, which come from an algorithm I developed based on my Ph.D. research at Stanford. The method takes margin of victory in games and accurately adjusts for strength of schedule. Let's look under the hood at how this works.

First, this method requires the margin of victory in every college basketball game before the tourney starts. This includes over 5,000 games each season.

Then, the method creates a network in which teams

are nodes and games are edges that connect these nodes. This was inspired by Google's PageRank algorithm, which brought order to the complex world of web search.

From this network, the method develops a set of equations to be solved. For college basketball before the 2015 tournament, there are 351 equations for 351 unknown variables, one for each team.

The method then solves for the over 300 variables at the same time, which requires more computer power than checking how often a 12 beats a 5 seed. The solutions to these equations give the team rankings in which the rank of each team depends on the performance of every other team in the network.

Each team gets its rank based on a rating, or an expected margin of victory against an average Division I basketball team. For any tourney game, the difference in the ratings of the two teams gives an expected margin of victory, or point spread.

The expected margin of victory implies a win probability for both teams. The win probability for a team to win the tournament comes from these game-by-game numbers.

How have these tourney win probabilities performed? For the 17-year period from 2002 through 2018, the team with the highest or next highest win probability by The Power Rank has won 9 of 17 tournaments. The win probabilities for these teams ranged from 32.2% for Kansas in 2008 *stdev?* to 13.2% for Florida in 2007.

These win probability calculations go beyond a team's rank and also consider the structure of the bracket. For example, Duke was the third ranked team heading into the 2015 tournament behind Kentucky and Arizona. However, three of the other top five teams, including Kentucky and Arizona, were on the other side of the bracket. Duke couldn't face these teams until the finals.

In performing the win probability calculation, Duke had a higher win probability than Arizona even though they had a lower rank. Duke had the easier path to the championship. *path*

Team-based college basketball analytics can help you make the most important decision of your bracket: which team to pick as champion. However, these win probabilities are not enough to win bigger pools. You need the right strategy. Let me explain.

2. The problem with picking favorites

It's easy to fill out your bracket with all the favorites. Head over to my site, ThePowerRank.com, and pick the higher ranked team in each game. Remember, the higher ranked team in pre-tourney rankings has won 71.2% of games from 2002 through 2018.

Most years, the bracket will look boring, and you might stab yourself in the eye from having to repeatedly cheer for teams like Duke and Kentucky. But we're here to win a pool, right?

Picking favorites gives you the best chance to win a small pool. However, it is not the best strategy for a medium sized pool, and it won't help at all for a large pool. Your chance to win a pool depends strongly on the size of the pool.

To understand the impact of pool size on your chance of winning, consider an analogy.

Drunks throwing darts at a dartboard

You and a friend walk into a bar and find the employees of a start-up company there. They have just secured their Series A funding from a venture capital firm and feel good about their future. In anticipation of becoming millionaires, they start throwing back flutes of Champagne.

After a few too many drinks, the workers from the company congregate near a dartboard. Against better judgment, they decide to play a game.

Each person gets one throw at a dartboard. Hit the bullseye and earn a free drink.

You laugh at the spectacle, thinking that not a single person will hit the bullseye. It doesn't matter that the bar has installed a magnetic field that directs all errant darts back toward the dartboard. Great for safety, but the bar still won't be serving up any drinks.

Your friend bets you that someone will hit the bullseye. Should you take the bet?

It depends on the number of people lined up to throw a dart. Let's assume that a dart from a drunk person has an equal chance of landing anywhere on the dartboard thanks to the magnetic field. The odds that any one drunk hits the bullseye is small, about 0.5%.

However, to win your bet, you need every drunk person to miss. There is a 99.5% probability that the first drunk misses, but you must multiply 0.995 by 0.995 to get the likelihood that both the first and second drunk miss. If the company has 20 drunks that step up to fling a dart, there's a 90.5% chance that all of them miss. This implies a 9.5% chance that at least one drunk hits the bullseye.

For an increasing number of drunks, the probability that at least one hits the bullseye increases rapidly. At 100, there's a 39.4% chance for someone to hit the bullseye, and this probability increases to 86.5% for 400 people.

The same principle applies to your March Madness pool. Suppose you're filling out a bracket in 2010. Kansas has just capped an amazing regular season and earned a 1 seed in the tourney. Analytics agrees with this assessment, as the Jayhawks top The Power Rank.

However, everyone in your pool has also picked Kansas. According to data from ESPN, 41.8% of brackets filled out on their site had Kansas as champion. If Kansas wins, you and many others get those 32 points.

However, just like the drunk people throwing darts, someone else in your pool will hit the bullseye in the earlier rounds. They will get lucky and pick two surprise Sweet 16 teams or a shocking Elite Eight team.

Only one person has to get lucky to topple you from the top of your pool. This gets more likely with more people in your pool.

How your chance to win depends on pool size

Let's put some numbers behind how your chance to win a pool depends on its size. This requires developing a simulation method that can account for two types of randomness in your pool.

Randomness in basketball games

First, the simulation must account for the inherent randomness in playing the game of basketball. In real life, the tournament only happens one time. In 2010, Kansas fell in the Round of 32 to Northern Iowa, and Duke went on to win the tourney.

However, if the same tourney happened again, the results would be different. Northern Iowa's Ali Faroukmanesh misses that three point shot, and Kansas survives and advances. Then maybe they beat Duke in the Final Four and win the tourney.

To handle this variance in basketball, the simulation uses my win probabilities at The Power Rank. For each game, a coin is flipped according to this win probability.

For example, if Kansas has a 97% chance to win their first game, this coin comes up heads on 97% of flips. Kansas advances on heads, but suffers an embarrassing, historic loss to a 16 seed on tails. By repeating this procedure for each game in each round, one can simulate the results of the tourney.

With modern computing, it's trivial to run 1,000 of these tourney simulations. For the 2010 tourney, Kansas would win in 311 of these simulations on average. Researchers use these types of "Monte Carlo" simulations to study phenomena ranging from polymer materials to the stock market.

Randomness in a pool

Second, there is variability among the brackets in your pool. A person in your pool might not know anything about college basketball and pick games depending on which mascot he likes.

Another person went to Connecticut as an undergrad and always picks the Huskies as champion. After Connecticut won two of four tourneys from 2011 through 2014 as a long shot, this person might not get invited back into the pool.

For the variability in brackets in your pool, we consult the data on brackets submitted to ESPN. To simulate a 50 person pool, the computer approximates 50 brackets at random from the millions submitted on ESPN. (If you want to get technical, the brackets generated by my simulation have the same statistics as the millions actually submitted. Since 41.8% of brackets had Kansas as champion in 2010, 41.8% of generated brackets will also have Kansas as champion.)

This is clearly an approximation to the actual brackets that might appear in your pool. For example, if you live in the state of Michigan, your pool will probably have more brackets with Michigan and Michigan State as champions than the national average. This can affect your choices, especially when we discuss contrarian strategies in the next section.

Pool win probability by picking favorites

For the 2010 tourney, I picked a target bracket in which the higher ranked team in The Power Rank won each game. This resulted in Kansas as champion.

Then I performed simulations at a number of different pool sizes and tracked the fraction of simulations in which the target bracket won. The results show how your chance to win a pool decreases rapidly with pool size for the 2010 tourney.

By picking all favorites, you have a 38% chance to win a 10 person pool. You'll win about every other year, which is pretty good. If winning is your only goal, enter a small pool.

For a 30 person pool, your chance of winning the pool drops to 16%. With your choice of Kansas as champion, there are enough others in your pool with this choice that someone else will win based on luck in picking earlier games.

In terms of investment potential, a win probability of 16% for a 30 person pool is pretty good. If you took a typical bracket from ESPN and submitted it, you would have the same chance as anyone else, or 3.3%, to win the pool. By submitting the favorites based on my numbers, you get a significant return on your investment. The public is like those drunk people throwing darts.

Pool win probability for picking favorites

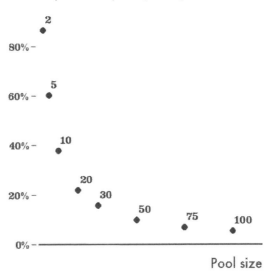

The visual shows your probability of winning a pool as a function of size for picking all favorites.

While this visual shows results for the 2010 tourney, the results look similar in all years.

However, the same tournament won't happen again next month. Even if you could get the same win probability every year, you're waiting about six years on average between winning pools.

For a 100 person pool, your probability to win a pool drops to 5%. A 400 person pool? I'm not even going to do the calculation. Don't enter a pool that big. Even with the best analytics, you'd be better off lighting your entry fee on fire.

Now let's look at how you can improve your chance of winning a bigger pool with a contrarian strategy.

3. Contrarian strategies, Part I

If you want to win an NCAA tournament pool, find a small pool with fewer than 10 people. By picking the higher ranked team in The Power Rank for each game, you have the best odds of winning since you avoid the randomness of bigger pools.

However, you probably won't do this. First, you have little control over the size of the pool. It's much easier to answer your friend's email than go in search of someone with a small pool.

Second, it's boring to enter a small pool. You get way more bragging rights by taking the top prize in a bigger pool.

You will most likely enter a bigger pool with more than 10 people. Fortunately, there's a strategy for increasing your odds of winning these medium sized pools. And surprisingly, it involves picking a champion with a lower win probability than the favorite.

To see why this works, let's examine your objective in filling out a bracket.

The contrarian approach to picking a champion

Consider these two different objectives you might maximize in filling out your pool:

- the expected number of points the bracket earns

- the probability of winning the pool

The calculations in this chapter show that these two goals are not the same and require different strategies.

To maximize the expected number of points your bracket earns, you can rely on accurate analytics. For example, consider a Round of 64 game in which Kansas has a 97% chance to win. This win probability implies that if Kansas played this game 100 times, they would win 97 of those games. On average, picking Kansas gets you 0.97 expected points, or 97 divided by 100. By picking Kansas's opponent, you get 0.03 expected points, not a wise move.

However, picking all favorites is not the best strategy for winning a medium sized pool. In most years, this requires picking the same champion as many other people in your pool. If this team wins the tourney, you get the 32 points for the correct choice of champion. However, many others also get these points.

The winner of the pool now comes down to picks in earlier rounds. With so many other people still in contention, one of them will get lucky with their picks. Think back to the likelihood that one drunk person hits the bullseye. The randomness from other brackets in your pool prevents you from finishing first.

Maximizing your chance of winning your pool requires not only analytics but the right strategy based on the bracket choices of others in your pool. While you can't just look at their brackets, the statistics that ESPN publishes on the millions of brackets submitted to their site allow for reasonable estimates.

With this information, you can make a contrarian choice for the tournament champion. You want to find a team that has a good chance to win the tourney but gets picked in few other brackets. If this team wins, you get 32 points that not many others will have. Your solid choices in earlier rounds based on analytics should secure the victory.

In this chapter, we look at how this contrarian strategy for picking a champion performs in a number of tourneys.

How to find a contrarian champion in 2010

Kansas entered the tournament as a huge favorite in 2010. Behind the dual threat Morris twins (Marcus and Markieff), the Jayhawks lost only twice the entire season.

Kansas had a 31.1% chance to win the tourney by my numbers, the best win probability by over 10%. However, the public knew the strength of these Jayhawks, as 41.8% of brackets submitted to ESPN picked them as champions.

The last chapter showed how your chance of winning a pool by picking Kansas as champion fell rapidly with pool size. For a 50 person pool, you had a 10% chance to win.

Instead of picking Kansas, you should find an overlooked team to pick as champion. In 2010, this contrarian choice was Duke. Usually a perennial contender to win the tourney, the Blue Devils looked down that season. They lost five times, including a bad 14 point loss at North Carolina State, a team that would end the season 20-16.

However, the numbers liked Duke. Despite the

losses, Duke was ranked second behind Kansas in The Power Rank heading into the tournament. My calculations gave them a 20.9% chance to win the tourney. Only 6.5% of public brackets had Duke as champion. Later, we'll see the importance of this big gap between win probability and public pick rate.

I performed simulations for both the favorites and contrarian strategies for different pool sizes. Since Kansas and Duke were the top two teams in my rankings, the switch between these strategies required only one change. The favorites bracket had Kansas as champion while the contrarian bracket had Duke as champion. Otherwise, the brackets were the same.

Picking the favorite Kansas as champion gave you the best chance to win small pools. For a 10 person pool, the choice of Kansas led to a 38% chance while Duke offered a 30% chance.

In 2010, the pool win probability for the favorites and contrarian strategies were equal for a pool size of 20. Both choices led to about a 20% chance to win a pool. For bigger pools, the contrarian strategy enjoyed an increasingly large edge over the favorites.

For example, the contrarian strategy with Duke as champion for a 50 person pool gave you a 14.8% chance to win your pool. Picking the favorites with Kansas as champion offered a 10% win probability. The contrarian strategy increased your odds by almost 50%.

Pool win probability

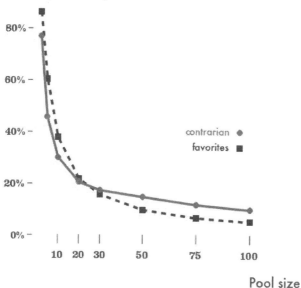

A comparison of picking favorites and the
contrarian strategy for the 2010 tourney.

However, the chance to win a pool with the contrarian strategy decreased with larger pools. Even with the right tactics, remember the first rule of winning a pool: Don't get in a big pool.

In the actual 2010 tournament, Duke made the Final Four but found none of the other pre-tourney favorites as their competitors. Kansas lost to Northern Iowa in the Round of 32, while Kentucky fell to West Virginia in the Elite 8. Syracuse fell victim to an upstart Butler team that wasn't even in the top 25 of The Power Rank entering the tourney.

Despite the lack of big name teams in the Final Four, Duke didn't just waltz to the championship. In the final against Butler, they had a one point lead in the final seconds with big man Brian Zoubek on the line. He made the first but missed the second free throw. Butler's Gordon Hayward scooped up the rebound, dribbled to half court and launched a shot.

If Hayward's shot drops, it's the greatest upset in the history of sports. Instead, it bounced off the backboard and rim to preserve a Duke win. It also most likely gave those who used the contrarian strategy of picking a champion a great chance to win their pool.

How to find a contrarian champion in 2012

For another example of the contrarian strategy, consider 2012, the year Amy Nelson made her *SB Nation* video on my analytics.

Kentucky - the Anthony Davis, Michael Kidd-Gilchrist version of John Calipari's NBA development team - entered the tourney as the huge favorite. My numbers gave Kentucky a 28.4% win probability while 35.1% of brackets chose them as champion.

With so many brackets picking the favorite as champion, I told Amy to make the contrarian choice.

Ohio State didn't seem like a title contender. Entering the tournament, they had 7 losses, and only 4.8% of brackets picked them as champion.

However, Ohio State played a difficult schedule that included Kansas and numerous strong teams from the Big Ten. My numbers rewarded Ohio State for this strength of schedule as they ranked second behind Kentucky in my pre-tourney rankings.

Ohio State had a robust 17.2% chance to win, so I told Amy to pick them as champion in the *SB Nation* video. In an ironic twist, Amy wore a Michigan shirt in parts of the video.

In the actual tourney, Ohio State made the Final Four and faced Kansas in the semi-final game. Ohio State led for most of the game, but Kansas made a late surge in the second half. Kansas sealed the victory when 6'0" Elijah Johnson made an off-balance layup over 6'8" Jared Sullinger of Ohio State.

Kentucky beat Kansas to win the tourney, and Amy didn't win her pool.

Back in 2012, I knew about contrarian strategy for picking a champion but didn't have the research to show that it worked. With my current methods, we can go back and analyze the choices made.

The simulations show that picking favorites gave the highest win probability for pools with fewer than 30 people. The contrarian strategy performed better for larger pools.

Amy was in a pool of 23 people, so Kentucky as champion gave her a slightly larger win probability. My simulations suggest she had about a 20% chance to win her pool.

However, even the choice of Kentucky would have put her fourth in her actual pool. The top seven brackets had Kentucky as champion, and the winner picked two unlikely Sweet 16 teams, Ohio and North Carolina State. A drunk hit the bullseye.

The contrarian strategy worked in 2010 but not in 2012. But these years had an important similarity: the contrarian choice had a much higher win probability than the fraction of the public that picked them.

In 2010, Duke had a 20.9% chance to win the tourney but only 6.5% of the public picked them. In 2012, Ohio State had a 17.2% chance to win the tourney but only 4.8% of brackets picked them.

Because of this large discrepancy, the contrarian strategy beats picking all favorites for pools as small as 25 to 30. For any pool larger than this cross-over size, you should use the contrarian strategy over picking all favorites.

However, the contrarian strategy doesn't always work for pools this small. Let's see why.

The contrarian champion in 2015

Kentucky was a clear favorite to win the 2015 tourney, and you didn't need analytics to figure that out. The Wildcats went undefeated before the start of the tourney, and they returned Mr. Clutch, Aaron Harrison. The previous season, Harrison hit late three point shots to beat Michigan and Wisconsin as 8 seed Kentucky made an improbable run to the title game.

With a deep and talented team, my numbers gave Kentucky a 35.9% chance to win the tourney in 2015. However, an astounding 48% of the public picked them as champion.

In 2015, the contrarian choice for champion was Duke, the third ranked team in my pre-tourney rankings. The Blue Devils had a 12.4% chance to win, a number enhanced by the structure of the initial tourney field. Duke could only meet Kentucky in the title game.

Based on ESPN's data, 9.3% of the public picked Duke as champion. Note this gap of 3% between my win probability and the public is much smaller than the gap for contrarian choices in 2010 and 2012.

Picking all favorites beats the contrarian strategy

for pool sizes up to almost 100. This results from the small gap between Duke's win probability and the public. However, the contrarian strategy is competitive with picking all favorites for pool sizes of 40 and greater.

In the actual tourney, Kentucky faced Wisconsin in a Final Four game. Even though Wisconsin entered the game as a 4.5 point underdog, they played one of their best games against Kentucky. Mr. Clutch couldn't save them this time, as Aaron Harrison's late three point shot during the last moments of the game didn't hit the rim. Kentucky lost and fell short of a perfect season.

In the final against Duke, it looked like Wisconsin would win going away as they had a nine point lead in the second half. Then Duke got an improbable 10 points from reserve guard Grayson Allen to close the gap. Duke held on in the final moments to give Coach K his fifth tournament title.

The contrarian approach benefited two readers of the initial version of this book. With Duke as the contrarian champion, Ryan Peters of Omaha, Nebraska, won a pool of size 100, the cross-over size at which the contrarian strategy starts to beat the favorites.

Max Rausch of San Francisco also won his competitive pool. He picked Duke over Kentucky and won a pool of size 40. He said, "I was a basketball novice in a crowd of 40 experts, so it was particularly satisfying."

In retrospect, the contrarian choice of Duke as champion didn't provide the highest win probability for a pool of size 40. Sometimes, going against the analytics works out in your favor.

The 2015 tourney was an extreme example for the cross-over from picking all favorites to the contrarian strategy. In 2009 and 2011, the contrarian choice of champion also had a win probability close to the fraction of the public that picked them as champion. Let's look at the cross-over pool size for these years.

In 2009, Connecticut had a 12.2% chance to win the tourney while 7.1% of public brackets picked them. The cross-over threshold was a pool size of about 45.

In 2011, Pittsburgh had a 11.2% tournament win probability while 6.2% of brackets on ESPN picked them as champion. The cross-over threshold was a pool size of 75.

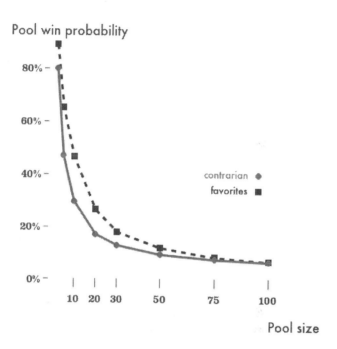

A comparison of picking favorites and the
contrarian strategy for the 2015 tourney.

In general, the contrarian strategy works best when the team's win probability greatly exceeds the public pick fraction. The high win probability gives you a better chance that the contrarian choice wins the tourney. The low public pick rate implies that not many others in your pool will get the 32 points when the contrarian team wins.

Contrarian champion as the favorite

Some years, the contrarian choice for champion has the highest win probability by my numbers. This situation provides an excellent opportunity to win your pool.

Consider the 2008 tournament. North Carolina started the season first in the AP rankings and lost only twice before the tournament. Led by Ty Lawson and Tyler Hansbrough, North Carolina had the support of the public, as 31.5% of brackets on ESPN picked them.

However, analytics favored Kansas in 2008. By margin of victory adjusted for strength of schedule, Kansas entered the tournament as the top team in The Power Rank. My numbers gave them a 32.2% chance to win the tourney.

For whatever reason, the public overlooked the traditional power Kansas in 2008. Perhaps the media focused more attention on North Carolina. Also, Kansas had three losses before the tourney compared with two for North Carolina and UCLA. On ESPN, 14.8% of brackets picked Kansas, less than the 31.5% and 19.2% for North Carolina and UCLA, respectively.

In the actual tourney, Kansas made the Final Four along with the other 1 seeds (North Carolina, UCLA and Memphis). They destroyed North Carolina to make the national championship game. But against Memphis in the final game, Kansas was down nine with 2:12 remaining in the second half.

Lucky for Kansas, Memphis missed four free throws in the last minutes of the game. This gave Kansas guard Mario Chalmers the opportunity to make a three point shot with 3.9 seconds remaining in the half to tie the game. His shot became an iconic tournament memory. Kansas prevailed in overtime to win the first national championship for coach Bill Self.

Kansas converted on their almost one in three chance to win the tournament in 2008, giving you a great chance to win your pool. However, a significant fraction of the public (14.8%) picked Kansas as champion, which still leaves you exposed to the luck of others. For a 50 person pool in 2008, I estimate a 17% win probability for a bracket that picks Kansas.

There were two other years in which the contrarian pick as champion also had the highest win probability: Florida in 2013 and Arizona in 2014. Neither of these two teams won the tourney.

How to find the contrarian champion

To find the contrarian champion, follow this simple three step process.

1. Check out my win probabilities at ThePowerRank.com, updated soon after release of the field on Selection Sunday. Find the team with the largest win probability.

2. For this team, compare its win probability with the fraction of brackets that pick this team as champion on ESPN. If this fraction is less than about 80% of its win probability, you have your value champion.

3. If this team does not meet this criterion, find the team with the next largest win probability and repeat the comparison in step two.

To find my team win probabilities and links to the public data, click here.

For seven of the eight years in which I've looked at the data, I found a value champion with a greater than 10% win probability but that was picked in fewer than 10% of public brackets. The only exception was 2008. While 14.8% of brackets picked Kansas, my numbers gave them a large 32.2% win probability.

4. Contrarian strategies, Part II

Let's review the three take-home messages from the research on winning your NCAA tournament pool.

1. You have the best chance to win a small pool with 10 or fewer people.

2. For larger pools, you need to pick a contrarian champion that has a large win probability but a small fraction of the public picking them. The larger the gap between these two numbers, the better this contrarian strategy works at smaller pool sizes.

3. Don't get in a large pool of over 100 people.

Armed with these basics, let's look at other considerations for filling out your bracket.

Contrarian choices in earlier rounds

The previous chapter introduced the contrarian choice for champion in your bracket. In the most common scoring system, the correct choice for champion is worth 32 points, one sixth of the total possible points and the most for any one game. Make this choice count.

However, correct picks for the two teams that play in the championship game are worth 16 points each. The correct choice of a Final Four team nets eight points. Can contrarian choices in these earlier rounds help your win probability?

To find out, let's go back to 2010.

Contrarian title game team in 2010

In the last chapter, we saw that Kansas entered the 2010 tourney as the public favorite but the smart bracket had Duke as the contrarian champion for bigger pools. This worked out well, as the Blue Devils won the tourney that year.

To find a contrarian choice for an earlier round of the tourney, we look to Syracuse. Jim Boeheim's team started the season with low expectations, as they didn't make the top 25 of the preseason AP poll. But with stellar play from Wes Johnson and Scoop Jardine, Syracuse went 28-4 and landed a 1 seed in the tourney.

However, not many had Syracuse in the championship game since they faced a possible Final Four game against Kansas, the public favorite. While 54.4% of brackets submitted to ESPN had Syracuse in the Final Four, only 18.1% picked the Orange to make the title game. Not many thought they could beat Kansas.

My numbers gave Syracuse a 25.8% chance to make the title game. This made Syracuse a contrarian choice to beat Kansas in the Final Four and play in the title game.

Now consider this double contrarian bracket: Duke as the value champion, and Syracuse as the contrarian choice to make the title game. Let's compare how this bracket does compared to the single contrarian bracket with Duke as champion.

For all pool sizes, the win probability is roughly the same for the single contrarian bracket with Duke over Kansas and the double contrarian with Duke over Syracuse.

For pool sizes between 10 and 30, the double contrarian bracket has a slightly larger win probability. However, I believe this results from the approximations I make in choosing public brackets at random.

To see why, I performed a number of studies of contrarian choices for the championship game and Final Four. In all cases, this choice didn't change the win probability as a function of pool size. This suggests that the 2010 results in which the double contrarian strategy performs better for pool sizes of 10 to 30 is a fluke.

Pool win probability

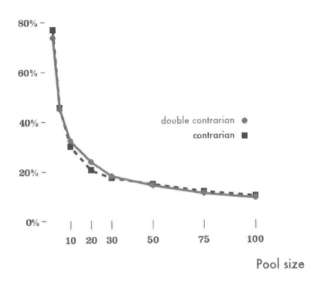

A comparison of the contrarian strategy and
the double contrarian strategy (championship and
semi-final game) for the 2010 tourney.

With these contrarian choices in earlier rounds, you take a small hit in the probability that you get this team correct. However, if your contrarian choice wins, you have an advantage on the competition, since not many others picked that team. These two effects seem to balance out and not affect your overall win probability.

In 2010, Syracuse didn't make the title game. In fact, Butler upset them in the Sweet 16 on their way to the title game. Duke survived a last minute shot by Butler to win the tourney.

Consider these two guidelines for making contrarian choices in earlier rounds.

First, use subjective factors to help make these contrarian choices in earlier rounds. In 2010, suppose you thought Syracuse had a good match-up against Kansas in a potential Final Four meeting. The research suggests your win probability doesn't change, so go ahead and make Syracuse the contrarian choice to play in the title game.

Second, contrarian choices in earlier rounds give you some freedom to submit a second bracket to your pool. For example, in 2010, you've already submitted a contrarian bracket with Duke as the champion over Kansas. As a second bracket, pick

Kansas as champion with Duke as the contrarian choice to make the title game. My numbers gave Duke a 37.7% chance to make the game, but only 17% of brackets picked them to go that far.

However, there's one thing you should not do in making contrarian choices. Let me use the 2012 tourney to explain.

How not to make contrarian choices

It's 2012, and Kentucky enters the tourney as the prohibitive favorite. Let's pick them as champion and look for contrarian choices in earlier rounds.

You think you see a juicy contrarian Final Four choice. No one, meaning only 3.9% of brackets, is picking Wisconsin to make the Final Four. However, the numbers say that the Badgers have an 8.3% chance to make the final weekend of the tournament.

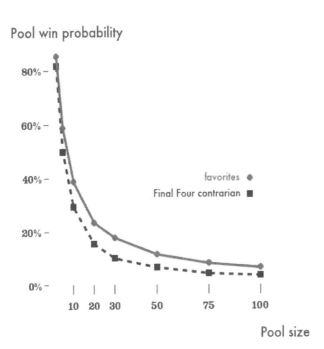

Pool win probability

A comparison of picking favorites and a bracket with a contrarian Final Four choice for the 2012 tourney.

With these contrarian choices in earlier rounds, you take a small hit in the probability that you get this team correct. However, if your contrarian choice wins, you have an advantage on the competition, since not many others picked that team. These two effects seem to balance out and not affect your overall win probability.

In 2010, Syracuse didn't make the title game. In fact, Butler upset them in the Sweet 16 on their way to the title game. Duke survived a last minute shot by Butler to win the tourney.

Consider these two guidelines for making contrarian choices in earlier rounds.

First, use subjective factors to help make these contrarian choices in earlier rounds. In 2010, suppose you thought Syracuse had a good match-up against Kansas in a potential Final Four meeting. The research suggests your win probability doesn't change, so go ahead and make Syracuse the contrarian choice to play in the title game.

Second, contrarian choices in earlier rounds give you some freedom to submit a second bracket to your pool. For example, in 2010, you've already submitted a contrarian bracket with Duke as the champion over Kansas. As a second bracket, pick

Kansas as champion with Duke as the contrarian choice to make the title game. My numbers gave Duke a 37.7% chance to make the game, but only 17% of brackets picked them to go that far.

However, there's one thing you should not do in making contrarian choices. Let me use the 2012 tourney to explain.

How not to make contrarian choices

It's 2012, and Kentucky enters the tourney as the prohibitive favorite. Let's pick them as champion and look for contrarian choices in earlier rounds.

You think you see a juicy contrarian Final Four choice. No one, meaning only 3.9% of brackets, is picking Wisconsin to make the Final Four. However, the numbers say that the Badgers have an 8.3% chance to make the final weekend of the tournament.

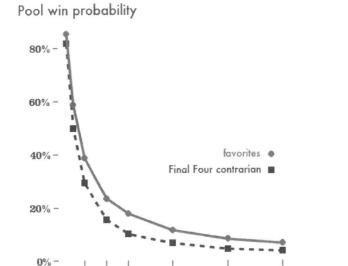

Pool win probability

A comparison of picking favorites and a bracket with a contrarian Final Four choice for the 2012 tourney.

2012 presents an example of how the initial field of teams affects your choices. Remember, Ohio State was the contrarian choice for champion that year. However, you can't pick Ohio State as champion if you make the contrarian choice of Wisconsin for the Final Four. Since these two Big Ten teams occupied the same region, only one of them could make the Final Four.

Wisconsin as a contrarian Final Four team greatly lowers your win probability for pools larger than 10. For example, picking all favorites gives you an 11.6% chance to win a pool of size 50. The same bracket with Wisconsin as a contrarian Final Four team has a 6.8% win probability.

Remember, the Badgers had an 8.3% chance to make the Final Four. If you picked teams at random to make the Final Four, Wisconsin would have a 6.3% chance (1 in 16).

It should be obvious, but don't make low probability contrarian choices. As a simple rule, the choice should have at least double the probability than picking a team at random.

Know who else is in your pool

The simulations in this book are based on public data on the brackets submitted to ESPN. I cannot stress enough that this is an approximation of the brackets that will actually appear in your pool. You might have to make subjective adjustments for the following criteria.

Geography

People pick their bracket based on their location and affiliations. For example, consider the 2010 tournament. We discussed that Duke was the contrarian team to pick as champion over the favorite Kansas. But the value of Duke depends on the assumption that few others in your pool will pick them as champions.

There are situations in which this assumption might be false. For example, if you're a Duke graduate and join a pool with other Duke alumni, there's a good chance that a reasonable number of people will pick Duke in your pool.

Small pools

The simulations in this book will better approximate reality for bigger versus smaller pools.

Because the simulation picks a bracket based on the public data at random, there is potential for small sample size effects in pools.

To understand this, consider the flipping of a coin with a 50-50 chance to land on heads or tails. If you flip a coin 10 times, you expect 50% of these tosses to land on heads. However, with such a small number of flips, there's a good chance you get only 3 heads or as many as 7 heads. (Feel free to find a quarter and try this.)

Instead, if you flip a coin 100 times, the chance that 30% of the tosses land on heads is much smaller. The law of large numbers, a fundamental result in probability, guarantees that the fraction of heads will be closer to 50% for 100 tosses than for 10. The fraction of heads will get even closer to 50% with more than 100 tosses.

When the simulation draws five brackets based on the public data, those five brackets might not look like the brackets in your pool. Be smart about this. If you enter a five-person pool with family members who think about college basketball once a year, you will have a great chance to win picking the favorites.

On the other hand, suppose you meet four guys at

the Sloan Sports Analytics Conference who make a living investing money in the college basketball betting markets. They seem like fun people because they invite you out to dinner at fancy Boston establishments like Grill 23. If they invite you into their March Madness pool, run the other way as fast as you can. My simulations will not reflect the brackets that end up in this pool.

5. Should you avoid picking three point shooting teams as champion?

By now, you know the most important bracket choice is champion. This pick earns you the most points, so focus your attention on teams that can win the tournament.

Can you get any extra edge in picking the champion? How about fading teams that shoot a lot of three pointers? With the single elimination structure of the tournament, a favorite can go ice cold from behind the arc and lose. You know the cliche: live by the three, die by the three.

The data seemed to support this hypothesis. In 2014, I looked at the three point shooting rates (number of three point attempts divided by total field goal attempts) for championship teams. Since 2002, only one champion (Florida in 2006) had a higher three point rate (34 percent) than the college basketball average (33 percent).

For awhile, this analysis made me look prescient. In a *Grantland* article before the 2014 tournament, I argued against a Villanova team that took 45 percent of their shots from three. They lost in the

Round of 32 as a 2 seed. The same advice applied the next year, and Villanova, this time a 1 seed, lost again in the Round of 32.

When the 2016 tournament came along, Villanova continued to live and die by the three. They took 44 percent of their field goal attempts from behind the arc. This strategy seemed particularly bad, as they only made 34 percent of their 3 point shots. Inside the arc, Villanova made 56 percent of their field goal attempts, sixth best in the nation.

Villanova won the 2016 NCAA tournament, as Kris Jenkins hit a three point shot to win the championship game over North Carolina. However, I wasn't back tracking on years of solid bracket advice just yet. In their last 5 games of the tournament, Villanova drastically reduced their three point rate and played to their strength of two point shots. Even better, they had the good fortune to make over half of their three pointers during this run.

Then Villanova won the tournament again in 2018. The Wildcats entered the tournament with a 47 percent three point rate. Luckily, I had dug further into the data on three point shooting by the time I sent out bracket advice that year.

This chapter reviews the argument for picking against three point shooting teams. Does the cliche *live by the three, die by the three* hold up by the data? If not, then why did no three point shooting teams win the tournament over a stretch of 12 years?

Team Williams versus Team Wright

The three point shot has a dramatic effect on basketball. Intuitively, it gives an underdog team a powerful weapon to defeat a much better team. Also, a favorite might lose if they can't make their usual percentage of three point shots.

To understand the importance of the three point shot, consider two teams. Team Williams, as in Roy Williams, only shoots two point shots and has a one half probability to make each shot. Team Wright, as in Jay Wright, takes only three point shots and hits one third of them.

If Team Williams and Team Wright play a game with 68 possessions and take one shot per possession, they will both score 68 points on average. However, they will not always score 68 points. Due to randomness, Team Williams scores 78 in some games but 62 in others.

Because of Team Wright's inclination for three point shots, they have a bigger spread in their point totals. In two of every three games, Team Wright will score between 56 and 80 points. In the math jargon, this means their point total has a standard deviation of 11.7 points. Team Williams, which only shoots two point shots, will have two thirds of their games land between 60 and 76, a smaller spread.

Favorites that shoot a high rate of three point shots have a larger spread in their point total, which makes them susceptible to upsets.

Variance in offensive performance

If teams that shoot a high rate of threes have a larger variance, this should appear in the data. Let's take a look.

At first, it seems reasonable to look at points per game and calculate the standard deviation in this quantity. However, this analysis is not ideal since teams play at different tempos. Team Williams takes advantage of every fast break opportunity and averages more than 70 possessions per game. Team Wright prefers the half court game and averages closer to 60 possessions per game.

To evaluate an offense, it's better to look at points per possession than points per game because the former accounts for tempo. In addition, the number of possessions in a game can be estimated based on the box score.

To count the number of possessions, consider the ways a possession can end. For example, a team can make a shot, which appears in the box score as field goals made. A team can also turn the ball over, and the box score tracks these turnovers (TO).

A team can also miss a shot. If the defense gets the rebound, the possession is over. If the offense gets the rebound, the same possession gets extended. For every missed shot that could end a possession, we need to subtract those not ended by an offensive rebound (OREB). Then the number of possessions from missed shots is field goals missed minus offensive rebounds.

Finally, a possession can end on free throws. If all free throws came in pairs as a result of shooting fouls, then the number of possessions would be half the free throw attempts (FTA). However, free throws can also come after made baskets, one and one situations and fouls on three point shots.

With these complexities, one must estimate the number of possessions that end in free throws from total attempts. Ken Pomeroy multiplies free throw attempts by 0.475 to get this number of possessions. Also, offensive rebounds on missed free throws extend the same possession, so these get subtracted from our estimate of possessions.

Putting this all together and noting that field goals made and missed equals field goal attempts (FTA), we get this formula for possessions.

$$\text{Possessions} = \text{FGA} + \text{TO} - \text{OREB} + (0.475 * \text{FTA})$$

A better estimate is obtained by performing this

calculation for both teams in a game and averaging the two numbers. A team's offensive efficiency is then points scored divided by this estimate of possessions.

With this definition, we can now calculate the variance in offensive efficiency. For the 2016-17 season, the figure shows how this variance changes with a team's three point rate (fraction of field goal attempts taken from three). Surprisingly, there is no statistical relationship between the two quantities. The data looks the same each season.

variance in
offensive efficiency

fraction of field goal attempts from three

So what's going on here? The original Team Williams versus Team Wright argument still holds, as three pointers increase the variance in points. Other factors must have a larger impact on the variance in offensive efficiency than three point rate. Let's speculate about two possible factors.

First, the randomness in making of three point shots plays a big role. While no one disputes the skill in shooting a basketball, Ken Pomeroy has shown that three point field percentage early in the conference schedule has little ability to predict the same quantity the remainder of conference play. The randomness in making three point shots has a clear impact on the variance in offensive efficiency.

Second, players do not perform at the same level each game. These hormonal teenagers get motivated to play rivals but then show a mediocre effort against other teams. Even Michael Jordan had his good and bad games.

The data show that three point rate doesn't affect the variance in offensive efficiency. A three point shooting team is no more likely to have an off night on offense than a team that takes more two point shots. As a result, do not avoid picking three point shooting teams as champion because of their three point rate.

So back in 2014, why didn't we see many tournament champions that shot a high rate of three pointers? To find the answer, let's dig into the evolution of college basketball.

Expected number of three point shooting champions

From 2002 to 2013, no tournament champion took a significant fraction of their field goal attempts from three. Florida in 2006 took 34 percent of their shots from three, the only champion higher than the 33 percent college basketball average over this period. But maybe we should not have expected any three point shooting teams to win.

To study this, I isolated teams that took over 40 percent of their shots from behind the arc and added up their win probability by my pre-tournament numbers. This sum gives the expected number of three point shooting teams to win.

From 2002 through 2013, this analysis gave 0.58 teams to win the tournament on average. With such a low expected number of champions, there is a reasonable probability that no three point shooting teams won the tourney over this 12 year period.

Repeating this analysis for 2014 through 2017, you get an additional 0.60 three point shooting teams to win the tournament. It was about equally likely to find a champion during this 4 year period as the previous 12 years. Villanova won in 2016, and college basketball produced the expected one three point shooting champion over 16 years.

In 2018, this analysis gave an expected 0.39 teams with a three point rate over 40 percent to win. In this single tournament, my numbers gave about two thirds the expected champions as the 12 year period from 2002 to 2014. Villanova fit this criterion, and they won their second championship in 3 years.

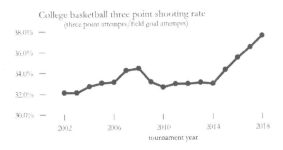

College basketball three point shooting rate
(three point attempts/field goal attempts)

College basketball has changed drastically from 2013 through 2019. In the 2013-14 season, 32.9 percent of field goal attempts came from behind the three point arc. Since that season, the three point shooting rate has increased by about one percent every season. Through mid-February of the 2018-19 season, the rate had increased to 38.6 percent.

The analytics revolution has played a role in this increased rate of three pointers. On average, a three point shot earned a team 5 more points per 100 shots than a two point shot during the 2017-18 season.

At least one program adopted the analytics right before the sharp increase in three point rate. In 2013, Sports Illustrated's Luke Winn reported that Villanova assistant coach Billy Lange did a study that showed the "value of three-point attempts."

That analysis led to a sharp increase in Villanova's three point rate and two NCAA championships.

New advice on three point shooting teams

Live by the three, die by the three. This old basketball chestnut seems to make sense, as the variance when taking a three point shot is larger than on a two. This suggests avoiding tournament champions with a high three point rate in your bracket.

However, this conventional wisdom breaks down at the game level. The data shows no relationship between a team's three point field goal rate and the variance in offensive efficiency over the course of a season. This suggests not picking against three point shooting teams as champion, and Villanova's titles in 2016 and 2018 support this.

In addition, the average rate of three point shots continues to increase in college basketball. With each passing year, more three point shooting teams will emerge as contenders to win the tournament. Do not avoid picking these teams because of their three point rate.

6. How often you win in the long run

You're excited to try out these contrarian strategies in your next pool. You can already imagine those bragging rights as you apply the concepts in this book year after year. However, I want to be completely honest about what your performance will look like.

Let's assume you get in a 30 person pool, a good situation for a medium sized pool. My calculations over previous years give a pool win probability between 12% and 20%. Let's take an optimistic scenario and assume an 18% chance.

On average, you'll win a pool about every five years. However, you don't just wait four years between each win. Randomness doesn't work like that.

To see what your year-by-year performance in pools might look like, I used my computer to flip a coin that comes up heads 18% of the time. The visual shows wins and losses for a 50 year period.

30 person pool with contrarian strategy:

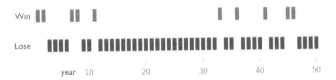

Just for the record, I only generated this sequence once. In no way did I generate sequence after sequence looking for one with streaks of wins and losses. They just happen due to randomness.

You win each of the next two years, and this book looks pretty smart. Through year 11, the contrarian strategies have won your pool five of 11 years.

However, remember the previous lesson about small sample size and the law of large numbers. When you have an 18% win probability, you will not continue to win almost half of your pools.

Starting in year 12, you don't win another pool for 21 years. Honestly, you probably gave up on my advice sometime during this stretch. And who can blame you for returning to randomly picking upsets? However, nothing changed about this coin flipping experiment after year 11. It gives an 18%

chance to win each year.

This streak of 21 years also sheds light on the idea of not picking high volume three point shooting teams from the last chapter. A long streak of failures doesn't mean an event will never happen or even has a low probability. Randomness is streaky, and it can fool us.

Luckily, you start using the contrarian strategies again in year 33. You win your pool five of the next 18 years. Over a 50 year stretch, you win exactly one in five pools.

I've tried to be honest about your chance of winning a pool. For a medium sized pool, this chance will most likely not exceed 20%, which will lead to long periods of not winning a pool. This will test your patience with the advice in this book.

However, if you apply these strategies year after year, you will come out ahead. Over this 50 year period, let's assume you paid a $10 entry each year and the winner takes all. For a total investment of $500, you won 10 pools for a total payout of $3000. Not a bad return on investment while enjoying the excitement of the tournament every year.

About the author

My name is Ed Feng, and I'm a data scientist and writer who specializes in football and March Madness predictions.

It all started in 2008. After reading an academic paper on Google's technology, I got inspired to apply my Stanford PhD to ranking sports teams.

My friends liked the resulting NFL rankings and encouraged me to do more. Now, hundreds of thousands of people each year look at my predictions at ThePowerRank.com.

In 2012, *SB Nation* made a video on my March Madness analytics. Later that year, my story predicting Alabama's win over Notre Dame in the college football title game appeared on the cover of *Sports Illustrated.*

My numbers and predictions have also appeared on *Deadspin*, *FiveThirtyEight*, and *Bleacher Report.*

Sign up for the free email newsletter

If you need accurate football and March Madness predictions, consider my free email newsletter.

I offer a sample of my college and pro football predictions usually reserved for paying members of my site. In addition, I keep you up to date on other content such as my preseason college football win totals report.

In addition, you get my March Madness cheat sheet every year with results optimal for a small pool.

Here's what Michael Sondag of Arlington, Va., says about the newsletter: "When I first thought about signing up, I was unsure about the content coming into my inbox. I didn't want spam. However, I found great and interesting content, catered at a frequency I enjoy. I particularly like the statistical analysis that challenges typical ways of thinking."

To sign up for this free service go to thepowerrank.com.

Made in the USA
Middletown, DE
13 March 2019